CW01657931

The
SPIRIT
of
PRAYER

AN END TIME MESSAGE

The SPIRIT *of* PRAYER

The Believer's Authority *on the* Earth

TOLULOPE OYEWOLE

Scripture quotations are taken from various translation of the Bible as indicated on the pages. All copyrights acknowledged. © February 2021, TAOO Publishing. All rights reserved. This book is subject to conditions that it shall not by way of trade or otherwise, be lent, resold, hired, reproduced in whole or in part in any form or otherwise circulated without the author's prior consent in any form of binding or cover other than that which it is published and without similar conditions being imposed on the subsequent purchaser. All rights reserved under international copyright law. All rights reserved, this book or any part thereof, may not be produced, stored in or introduced into a retrieval system, or transmitted, in any form or by any means electronic, mechanical, photocopy, recording or otherwise without the written permission of the publisher.

Paperback ISBN: 978-1-5272-8550-7
e-Book ISBN: 978-1-8384284-0-2

Published by TAOO Publishing

DEDICATION

To everyone who has lost a loved one due to the COVID-19 pandemic that has ravished the world. I pray that the peace and comfort of God will garrison your mind and hearts in these dark and trying times.

To my lovely wife–Debbie Oyewole, who has always been a source of comfort and joy to me and everyone around us. I am glad to spend forever with you under the Lordship of our Lord Jesus Christ.

To my lady, the bride of my Lord, to whom I am called to be a Prophet and an Evangelist in this generation.

CONTENTS

FOREWORD

I believe I'm not alone when I say that there are seasons in my life when my prayers lose their efficacy. I pray when I awake in the morning, with my children over meals, and as a family before bedtime. It happens so often that, at times, I don't think deeply about it. If I or someone close to me experiences hardship, of course my prayers are fervent for a time, but I soon fall back into my usual routine. It takes a new viewpoint or a shared story to remind us why we pray, the strength it can give us, and how it can bring the power of God into our lives.

That's what Tolu Oyewole offers us in this book. Through scripture, he explores the deeper meaning and power we can find in prayer and reminds all Christians of their calling to the divine work of prayer. We are the Lord's hands on earth. We need the connection Tolu describes to access the Lord's will. We need the authority prayer provides us to work the Lord's will in our lives and the lives of those around us—our families, our friends, our communities, and even our nations. Tolu's words will wake you to a renewed desire to fully utilize the power of prayer in your life.

—Katie Stirling

APPRECIATION

I am grateful to God my Father, for gracing me with this message to bring to His Church at this time. This has by far been the most difficult book I have had to write, and it is my prayer that I have done as instructed and not missed His will at any point in the journey of producing this message. And if I have, I pray that His truth will eclipse our hearts.

I am grateful for the love, support and contribution of my wonderful wife, Debbie Oyewole. She has indeed been a rock and a source of encouragement to me. I look forward to forever with you.

I am grateful for my close friend and brother, Dare Oduale for taking the time to challenge me on some of the truth presented in this book. Your support and insight was invaluable.

I am grateful to my team who worked tirelessly in the background to help me bring this book to you. They are Dare Oduale, Olanrewaju Fasoranti (marketing lead), Alan Dino Hebel of Book Designers for the quality delivery of the book design, my mentee Samuel Iyinkanmi – the Timothy to my Paul (for the technical support at my book launch), my editors – Katie Starling and Verity Casey.

I am also grateful for all the ministers who have partnered with me to ensure that this book gets to you. These include: Pastor Kolade Adebayo-Oke, Pastor

Yomi Odukoya, Pastor Sam Baptist, Pastor Damilola Ogunlade, Minister Tobi Olujinmi, Minister Tobiloba and Minister Taiwo Osuntuyi - I am really grateful to you all.

I would like to acknowledge my local Church–the New Covenant Cherubim and Seraphim Church, especially the Youth of Covenant and Light of Christ Ministries–a group of dynamic young people I am deeply proud of. These are men and women of God who are truly inspirational; they are indeed the best team I have ever been privileged to work with.

I am grateful for my SAGE (Saving a Generation Endangered) bible group. You all have been a source of joy to me and my family. I am especially grateful to Tobi Olujimi, who serves as our leader, and Pastor Adebayo-Oke (aka Chief), who serves as our Pastor and father.

Last but not the least; I am grateful for my family–both the Oyewole and Shobo families, for your constant support and prayers. I love you all!

PREFACE

In my last book, *And They Shall Be Called the Sons of God*, I discussed the purpose of the Christian on the Earth, based on Psalm 82. As a recap—God has placed us as Christians to stand as the Light and Salt of the Earth. Therefore, it is our divine duty to rise and combat the evil and redeem the desolate heritages that have been destroyed by darkness.

Satan is looking to build a kingdom on God's Earth to spite God, and he is doing this by lording over humans, who were assigned by God to rule the Earth (Psalm 115:16). The reason Jesus came was to deliver us from Satan's tyranny and bring us back into our inheritance by creating a new type of man—the Christian. Everyone who believes in the work of Jesus has been brought into their inheritance and been given authority over the Earth through the name of Jesus. However, Satan is still lording over the Earth because he has the majority of humanity deceived. The Christians who have been tasked to free the remainder of humanity do not know who they are, what their authority is, or how to use it.

And They Shall Be Called the Sons of God aimed to establish the identity and authority of the Christian on the Earth. In this book, *The Spirit of Prayer: The Believer's Authority on the Earth,* we will explore how we can effectively exercise the authority we have available to us in Christ Jesus. Christians will come to understand when it is appropriate to make decrees in the place of prayer, or to make petitions to God. Therefore, this book can be seen as a sequel to the last. While it is not imperative to read the former, this book may be understood more fully in the context of it.

Chapter 1
A CALL TO PRAYER

Therefore I exhort first of all that supplications, prayers, intercessions, and giving of thanks be made for all men, for kings and all who are in authority, that we may lead a quiet and peaceable life in all godliness and reverence. (1 Timothy 2:1–2 NKJV)

God is calling every Christian to pray. There is a spirit of prayer that has been released on the Earth by God as we wade through the last days. The darkness in the world thickens as Satan and his angels set the scene for their new world order. God is counting on the Church—the Body of Christ—to stop Satan in his tracks so that he (Satan) does not enact his plan before his time.

The spirit of prayer does not imply that there is a spirit called 'Prayer'. However, it suggests that God has impressed a burden on the hearts of those who are open to Him, to pray. It is God's call to His Children to rise and exact His power on the Earth through prayer.

The Meaning of Prayer

Prayer can be defined as a request, petition or thanks, addressed to God or other deities. It is an activity performed as a religious ritual by all forms of religions.

However, for the Christian, prayer is more than a request or ritual performed to please God. Jesus taught His disciples not to pray with vain repetitions and babbling because the Gentiles felt their prayers would be heard by much speaking (Matthew 6:7). It is important to remember that the Kingdom of God is not about speaking, but the demonstration of power (1 Corinthians 4:20). Therefore, there needs to be intentionality to prayer for it to be effective.

Several Christian ministers define prayer as having a conversation with God, or positioning ourselves to have an encounter with God. These definitions are true, but they are limited. As a maturing Christian, I used to think that the scriptural admonition to pray without ceasing meant always being in fellowship with God. This is still true, but it is a limited truth. Fellowship with God is not an end in itself, though it is very wonderful and extremely important. Hearing from God is not an end, it is a means to end.

In the scriptures we see that many people heard from and had great fellowship with God, but the result of their fellowship was a demonstration of His authority in the regions God assigned to them. Remember, Paul told the Corinthian Church that the Kingdom of God is not about talking. This, therefore, means that God does not talk in vain. He speaks for a reason and with an intended purpose. Thus, it is not so much what God says to you that matters, but rather, what you do as a result of what He said.

Let's take Moses for example (Exodus 14). God told Moses in the place of prayer not to take the children of Israel through the eleven-day journey route, but to take them to camp at the bank of the Red Sea. He said that He would harden Pharaoh's heart to pursue the children of Israel so He could destroy Pharaoh and his army. Moses responded in obedience, but when the manifestation of God's word came and the army of Egypt was closing in on the children of Israel, they began to panic. Moses tried to console them with words of exaltation. When Moses lifted his hands to prayer, God told him not to cry to Him, but to stretch out his hands and divide the sea.

Understand what God is teaching us here. Moses had already prayed, and in the place of prayer, God had shown Moses His will and what to do. What was left was for Moses to do as directed by God. When Moses stretched out his hands, the Bible tells us that God blew a great wind from His nostrils and divided the sea.

Let's review what happened here:

1. Moses prayed and discovered the will of God.

2. Moses prayed and exacted authority over the situation through the demonstration of the power of God.

It was not enough to know what God was saying. Moses had to bring it to pass by His power.

Another example is Elijah (1 Kings 17–18), who

lived at a time when the children of Israel were given to sin and were led by one of the most wicked kings to ever ascend the throne of Israel—Ahab. In the place of prayer, Elijah discovered it was the will of God to shut the Heavens for three and a half years so that there would not be rain in Israel, as judgement for their wickedness. Elijah appeared before Ahab to declare the news, and so began the drought and famine. However, when it was time for God to visit the land and bring back the rain, the Bible tells us that Elijah pressed in the place of prayer until he got confirmation from God and declared that rain would come again to the land. Just as with Moses, Elijah heard from God in the place of prayer, and through prayer, displayed the will of God.

The Bible also tells us that Jesus rose early in the morning to pray—before the sun—and the next thing we saw Him doing was cast out demons and heal the sick (Mark 1 35–39).

Therefore, prayer is an intentional_act of fellowship with God, through which we discover His will and exact His authority on the Earth by the demonstration of His power and excellence. Hence, the call of God discussed in this book is not for an increase in religious activities, vain repetitions and babblings. It is a call to know the will of God for your life and the region He has assigned to you. It is a call to bring to pass His will, by exacting His divine authority through the demonstration of His power, just as Moses, Elijah and Jesus did.

The question, therefore, is how do we access this

new level of prayer? We only have access once we, as the Body of Christ, understand our position in Christ Jesus. Until we know exactly what the Church is and who we are as Christians, we cannot fully function in the heritage that God has delivered to us, through the work of Christ on the cross, His resurrection from the dead and ascension to the Heavens.

Chapter 2

THE HEROES OF GOD

And God raised us with Christ and seated us with him in the Heavenly realms in Christ Jesus. (Ephesians 2:6)

As Christians, God has called us to be His heroes and the saviours of the Earth. Several years ago, the Lord Jesus appeared to me in a night vision. He appeared as the captain of the Lord's Army—in the form of a superhero—and told me I am to be His witness. Oh, what a wonderful day that was! Jesus Christ is leading a band of heroes called to save the Earth from the power of darkness. This is the same calling Paul received when Jesus commissioned him to the Gentiles. Paul was called to deliver them from darkness and bring them into the light; to deliver them from the power and bondage of Satan into the power of God (Acts of the Apostles 26:18). We too, have received the same calling for the regions God has assigned to each of us.

In my book, *And They Shall Be Called the Sons of God*, I explained that God has called us as the Church to restore the desolate heritages of the Earth to the dominion of God. From the time Adam and Eve sinned, the Earth was placed under a curse. As Christians, the death of Jesus Christ on the cross and His resurrection from the dead, has delivered us from the curse that came to the world as a result of Adam's disobedience; and consequently, from the tyranny of Satan.

The Position of the Church

Psalm 82 shows us that God is calling the members of His Church to take their place as gods of the Earth. When Jesus rose from the dead, He proclaimed that all power and authority in Heaven and the Earth had been given to Him. Therefore, our role as the Church is to enforce the authority of the Lord Jesus on the Earth.

The Prophet Isaiah explains this in Isaiah 53 8&10–NIV:

> *For he was cut off from the land of the living; for the transgression of my people he was punished ...and though the LORD* makes his life an offering for sin, *He will see His offspring and prolong His days, and the will of the LORD* will prosper in His hand.

The Church is that offspring. We are the continuation of the life of Christ on the Earth. Just as Jesus gave glory to the Father by fulfilling His will of revealing His identity and bestowing His glory to those who would come to believe in Him and become a member of His Body, so are we to give glory to God by demonstrating His glory, dominion and power—through the place of prayer.

When Jesus gave His final account to God in John 17, He told God that He wants us to be where He is. But He also mentions that He is not asking that God should take us out of this world. This statement indicates that Jesus was not talking about Heaven. He was not speaking of a geographical connotation, but rather referring to a position. The question thus becomes: Where was Jesus going? At the beginning of the account, Jesus asked the Father to restore Him to the glory they once shared. This means that Jesus was to be restored to the throne of God, just as He was, before He—the Word—became flesh and dwelled amongst men. We see this prayer answered when the Apostle Paul states in his letter to the Ephesian Church that God raised us together with Christ and seated us far above principalities and powers (2:6). This indicates that the authority Jesus has belongs to the Church. Paul's epistle to the Romans states we are joint heirs with Christ (8:17). This means we own it in the same way that He does. What does this mean for us today?

To understand this, we need to understand why Jesus came. When Adam sinned, he gave the world over to Satan, who became the god of the world. Jesus came as the second Adam to ransom the world from the hands of Satan, and He has now been installed as the God of Heaven and Earth and the King of Glory.

However, Jesus has now gone to Heaven to reign from there. How will the world know that Satan has been dethroned, and he is no longer their god? This is where the Church comes in. We are to reign as Christ on the Earth. This is why Jesus was sent to us—the Church—the person of the Holy Spirit. We have the fullness of God in the Church in the Holy Spirit. Therefore, we have the authority to reign as Christ—the second Adam.

The Church is supposed to be the most influential entity throughout the world, because we are Christ, the God of this world. Nothing should happen on the Earth without our permission and authorisation. Jesus confirmed this to His disciples when He told them that whatever they permit on the Earth will be permitted in Heaven, and whatever they bind on the Earth will be bound in Heaven (Matthew 18:18). By this, Jesus was revealing our authority in His name. Whatever decisions we make will be backed up by Him in Heaven, because He is the One deciding for us on the Earth. This promise was not just to His disciples of that time. The promise is true for us today. We just need to wake up to this revelation and the responsibility that comes with it.

Sadly, in most cases, the Church has not grown into her inheritance. We are like the child who owns the entire estate but still takes orders and direction from the help. We need to wake up and realise that they all work for us. In our ignorance, Satan has continued his rule as the rebel power holder, but it is time for us to exact our dominion and restore the desolate heritages of the world. It is time for us to constrain the influence of Satan over the world. God said in Psalm 82:6 that we are gods. It is time for us to take our place and defend the defenceless, help the needy and deliver those who have been taken captive. We are called to be the saviours of the world, by demonstrating the salvation that Jesus has brought to the Earth through His death on the cross and His resurrection from the dead. We do this in the place of prayer. However, to pray effectively, we need to understand our enemy.

Chapter 3

KNOW THE ENEMY

For we do not wrestle against flesh and blood, but against principalities, against powers, against the rulers of the darkness of this age, against spiritual hosts of wickedness in the Heavenly places. (Ephesians 6:12)

The first thing every Christian must come to terms with very early on in their faith, is that we are at war. There is a rebel force who knows it has been defeated but is keen on maintaining its influence on the world, even though this influence is now being held illegally. However, we are not at war with flesh and blood—that is, with human entities—even though they are used in this warfare. We are at war with spirit beings. They are called Principalities, Powers, Rulers of Darkness and Spiritual Wickedness in Heavenly Places (Ephesians 6:12).

The question therefore, is who are these Satanic entities and how do we address them? In my last book, I described who these beings are. After conducting further studies on the subject, I will endeavour to give a more detailed description of these entities, especially relating to prayer and Christian warfare. However, before going into the details, here is a snapshot of the Satanic hierarchy, culled from my last book:

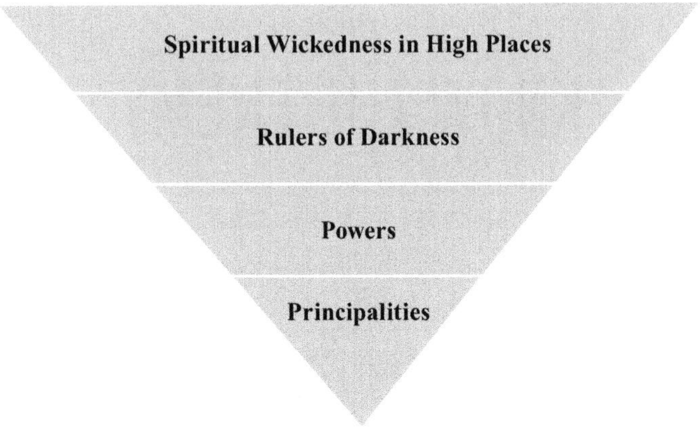

Spiritual Wickedness in High Places

These entities are the ruling body of Satan's Kingdom, and they operate from the Heavens. They are princes of darkness, a Satanic brotherhood that has made a pact to take forceful dominion of God's creation under Satan's leadership. They are the ones who rule the affairs of men and work to resist the God's plans on the Earth on a global scale. They are described as thrones (Colossians 1:16), dominions (Ephesians 1:21) and were very high-ranking angels in God's Heaven. From my study on this subject, it is my opinion that the following constitute this super sect of Satanic rulers:

- Satan—the leader
- Death
- Hell
- Famine

- Pestilence
- Abaddon—the Prince of Egypt
- The Prince of Assyria
- The Prince of Babylon
- The Prince of Persia
- The Prince of Greece—the spirit which I believe will be behind the Anti-Christ (Daniel 6:6; Revelations 13:2)

While I don't believe that this is an exhaustive list, I have listed them here so we can easily identify their activities on the Earth and know what we need to do to stop them in their tracks.

Rulers of Darkness

As explained in my previous book, Rulers of Darkness are spirit beings who have dominion over significant areas of the world for a set period. I believe that these rulers are not lower than Spiritual Wickedness in High Places, but are a devolved version of them. Certain entities of the Spiritual Wickedness group are assigned to reign as Rulers of Darkness in regions that have major influence in the world's political and economic scene. For example, Jesus indicated in Luke 10:18 that He saw Satan fall to the Earth like lightning. Many Christians and Bible scholars have interpreted this to mean Satan's displacement from Heaven and his inability to go back into Heaven to accuse the saints before God, as he did with Job. This notion is wrong on two counts:

1. Satan was already displaced from God's Heaven even before Adam was created on the Earth.

2. Satan was able to access God's presence during the time of Job with the Adamic authority he stole when he deceived Adam. That authority could have only been revoked when Jesus faced Satan as the second Adam and displaced him as the God of this world by recovering the Adamic authority that he stole. This was achieved when Jesus died on the cross, descended to Hell and rose from the grave. It was only at this point that Satan lost the Adamic authority and no longer had access to God's presence to accuse the saints.

Therefore, Satan did not fall from Heaven as a sign of defeat. No, he came down to the Earth to set up his throne and oppose Jesus and those that would believe in Him. Later on, in the book of Revelations 2:13, Jesus revealed to John that Satan's throne was established in Pergamum. This was not figurative or an allegory—it was literal. Satan's throne was there. This is why I believe that Satan was the Prince of Darkness ruling over the Roman Empire, perhaps this is why the emperors ascribe divinity to themselves, because they were under the influence of the being with the biggest god complex in the entire universe.

We see another example of this in Ezekiel 28, where Ezekiel is asked to take up a lamentation for the King of Tyre:

> *You were the seal of perfection, full of wisdom and perfect in beauty. You were in Eden, the garden of God; every precious stone adorned you: carnelian, chrysolite and emerald, topaz, onyx and jasper, lapis lazuli, turquoise and beryl. Your settings and mountings were made of gold; on the day you were created they were prepared.*
>
> *You were anointed as a guardian cherub, for so I ordained you. You were on the holy mount of God, you walked among the fiery stones. You were blameless in your ways from the day you were created till wickedness was found in you.*
>
> *Through your widespread trade, you were filled with violence, and you sinned. So I drove you in disgrace from the mount of God, and I expelled you, guardian cherub, from among the fiery stones. Your heart became proud on account of your beauty, and you corrupted your wisdom because of your splendour. So I threw you to the Earth; I made a spectacle of you before kings. By your many sins and dishonest trade, you have desecrated your sanctuaries.*
>
> *So I made a fire come out from you, and it consumed you, and I reduced you to ashes on the ground in the sight of all who were watching. All the nations who knew you are appalled at you; you*

> *have come to a horrible end and will be no more.* (verses 12–19 NIV)

This scripture is describing Satan as the King of Tyre. Therefore, Satan was again, at this time, the Prince of Darkness ruling over this nation, which had significant economic power during the time of Ezekiel. This indicates that at diverse times, Satan himself rules over certain areas of the world and uses that region for global influence. This same principle and blueprint are carried out by this brotherhood of darkness under the leadership of Satan. The rulers of darkness are:

- Satan—the Prince of the World, Rome, Tyre
- Abaddon—the Prince of Egypt
- The Prince of Assyria
- The Prince of Babylon—according to Revelations, this is the Prince of Darkness that will usher in the reign of the Anti-Christ
- The Prince of Persia
- The Prince of Greece—according to Revelations, this Prince of Darkness will be the spirit working in the Anti-Christ, which will be empowered by the Devil

These dark princes partner with their other comrades in the Spiritual Wickedness group to amplify their reign on the Earth, according to plans of Satan. For example, the COVID-19 pandemic is a function of pestilence. However, some Bible leaders believe that the dark prince responsible for the infrastructure to leverage the COVID-19 pandemic is the Prince of Assyria. This notion is based on Isaiah 10:13–14 (NKJV):

> *For he says: 'By the strength of my hand I have done it, And by my wisdom, for I am prudent; Also I have removed the boundaries of the people, And have robed their treasuries; So I have put down the inhabitants like a valiant man. My hand has found like a nest the riches of the people, And as one gathers eggs that are left, I have gathered all the earth; And there was no one who moved his wing, Nor opened his mouth even a peep.'*

The description painted in the scripture above reflects how the economies of the world have been destroyed. Therefore, I believe that the dark prince that inspired and influenced the king of Assyria, and made him proud in his heart, is the same dark prince responsible for the description of the world through this pandemic.

His objective is to create a world ready for the Anti-Christ before the time set by God—to extend Satan's reign of dominion beyond the plan of God. His mode of operation is to destroy borders through widespread state capture and to subjugate political leaders by deceiving them to sign laws that will rob them of their political powers and erode the human rights of their citizens.

If you have been following the news, you will realise that most political leaders, regardless of their political party association, are following the same script; even the media seems to be guilty of this.

Powers

These demonic authorities rule over nations or institutions that have similar powers or influence as nations—such as international organisations, professional institutions and secret cults. These Satanic entities report directly to Prince of Darkness over them. We see this, for example, in the vision of Daniel when the Angel Gabriel visited him:

> *Then he said to me, 'Do not fear, Daniel, for, from the first day that you set your heart to understand and to humble yourself before your God, your words were heard, and I have come because of your words. But* ***the prince of the kingdom of Persia*** *withstood me twenty-one days; and behold, Michael, one of the chief princes, came to help me, for I had been left alone there with* ***the kings of Persia.***' (Daniel 10:12–13 NKJV)

In this scripture, we see two entities: the Prince of Persia and the Kings of Persia. In this context, the Prince of Persia refers to the Prince of Darkness over Persia, and the kings refer to the Powers that have been given dominion in the regions that are under the control of the Kingdom of Persia. These Powers are subservient to the Prince of Persia.

If you study some of the modes of operations of certain institutions like the International Monetary Fund, World Bank or the World Health Organisation, you will see that they usually mirror the ideals and policy of the International Community, which is led by the United States. Perhaps this is why the President of the United States also holds the title 'Leader of the Free world'. Therefore, it seems to follow that the Prince of Darkness over the United States is also responsible for controlling the Powers of these institutions.

Principalities

These are municipal spiritual authorities ruling over local areas that are empowered by the Powers over those regions. They are responsible for frustrating the progress of God's kingdom in their region and holding the people living in that region in darkness. Some principalities have also been assigned to local communities and even families. Therefore, you see certain families exhibit some ungodly characteristics that are specific to them, or repeatedly experience unexplainable unfortunate circumstances, consistent with all the members of their family.

Why Is This Important?

This is important because we need to identify the entities we are dealing with to know how to address them. In the spiritual realm, insight is gold. If you do not know what you are dealing with, in most cases you may not see the desired result. For example, when David Yonggi Cho started his Church in South Korea, he struggled to connect to the people. Today he has arguably the biggest congregation in the world. The secret to his breakthrough is that he was confronted by the Principality over that region in a dream and defeated it. In the same vein, most ministries will continue to struggle to do the things God has called them to do if they do not first conquer the spiritual forces operating in those regions. Jesus said that until you bind the strong man, you cannot take his spoils (Mark 3:27). These spiritual entities have been set as strong men over certain regions of the Earth at different levels. Therefore, we need to identify and bind them to bring relief to those they have held in captivity. This is why the Bible says that even the captive of the mighty shall be set free (Isaiah 49:25). These Satanic entities are 'the mighty' referred to in this scripture, and we are the ones God will use as His battle axe to set them free—through prayer.

Another reason it is important to know this, is because these spiritual entities use men and women as fronts and conduits. The Lord told me many years ago that both He and Satan can only influence the

Earth through the agency of man. The reason Satan can still claim to be the prince and god of this world is that he has a majority of humans under his influence, especially in places of power. This is why the role of secret societies is very important in Satan's grand plan of world domination. In local regions, some sorcerers or priests represent these entities and use their powers to hold the region captive. We see this example with Elymas and Simeon in the book of the Acts of the Apostles. They were both sorcerers who used their demonic powers to torment their region. We need to know this because sometimes we will have to deal with the spirit operating behind the man before the man can be dealt with. Therefore most Christians and ministries are at a disadvantage when facing spiritual battles, because they are unaware of the spiritual entities involved and how to address them. It is important to note that whatever we see in the physical is controlled from the spiritual realm. So the first port of call when dealing with difficult situations or people is to bind the spirit involved in the place of prayer, before addressing the humans involved.

However, the ranking of the enemy we are dealing with will determine how we need to address our adversary in prayer. There are some which a single Christian can easily cast out, and there are others (who are very high ranking), that require the whole Church to pray for them to be defeated. It is for this reason that the Church, as a collective, needs to understand our authority and jurisdiction in the realm of the spirit. If we do not know this, we will continue to live as captives, even though God has called us—the Church—to be the saviours of the Earth.

Chapter 4

THE BELIEVER'S AUTHORITY

The heaven, even the heavens, are the LORD*'s;*
But the earth He has given to the children of
men. (Psalm 116:15 NKJV)

Think of a police officer when she orders a car to stop. Does the police officer have the physical power to stop the car? Of course not. However, the police officer has the authority to stop the car because of the power of the law. In the same vein, Christians have authority on Earth, because of the power of God in us.

However, a police officer can only attest to and exercise the authority she has if she can identify herself as a police officer through her uniform or badge, proving her identity, as well as other tools such as a gun, taser, handcuffs or baton. Therefore, authority is a combination of identity and tools of enforcement. Similarly, the Christian needs to be able to identify herself as a Christian and exercise the tools of warfare provided to her in Christ Jesus. In my previous book, I spoke about the identity of the Christian, and how we can operate in our identity. In this book, I will discuss the tools available to us to exercise our authority on the Earth.

The Weapons of Our Warfare

Unlike the police officer, we do not fight physical battles. Therefore, the weapons of our warfare are not physical. Paul in his second letter to the Church at Corinth advised:

> *The weapons we fight with are not the weapons of the world. On the contrary, they have divine power to demolish strongholds. We demolish arguments and every pretension that sets itself up against the knowledge of God, and we take captive every thought to make it obedient to Christ* (2 Corinthians 10:4–6 NIV).

These weapons are encapsulated in prayer.

Jurisdiction

Police officers are not the only enforcement agents in a society. Many other agents have assigned jurisdiction. For example, in the United States, local police forces deal with the enforcement of state laws. A police officer operating under the credentials of the New York Police Department will require permission to operate in another state. However, state police cannot enforce federal laws; this falls under the jurisdiction of the FBI. In spiritual matters, the Church has jurisdiction and so does the individual Christian. Understanding this truth will help the Christian and the Church understand when to make decrees and when to make petitions.

Jurisdiction of the Church

Jesus said to His disciples, 'Again, truly I tell you that if two of you on Earth agree about anything they ask for, it will be done for them by my Father in Heaven. For where two or three gather in my name, there am I with them'. (Matthew 18: 19–20 NIV)

Jesus was describing here the authority of the Church on the Earth. He was not just referring to the people listening to Him at the time, but to all that would come to believe in His name. The Church has the authority to influence activities on the Earth. When we, as the Church, gather in agreement, we have the power to change laws, demonic principalities and powers, and halt the activities of darkness on the Earth. We have the authority to decree changes and fight for those who are being oppressed by the wickedness of men. The only clause here is that we have to agree. Why is there so much discord in the Body of Christ? The strategy of Satan is to reduce our authority by dividing us. There is something about the gathering of men in agreement that makes the impossible possible. Satan knows this, and that is why he is consistently working to bring the human race to agree with him. He is working to build the New World Order, just as he attempted to do when men gathered to build a city and a tower that would reach the Heavens. God had to scatter mankind to prevent Satan from building his kingdom on the Earth and taking dominion over the affairs of men (Genesis 11). This has always been the strategy of Satan: to build a one-world system. He started in the days of Nimrod and continued in all the empires that arose throughout history. Satan understands the great power that is available if men work in agreement, and he wants that power to work for him. Therefore, he will do everything he can to oppose the Church and ensure we do not work together.

I feel so sad that, in many cases, Satan has worked unopposed because the Church is not in agreement. The appointed leaders of Churches seem to be only interested in building their empire, instead of the Kingdom, in the guise of doctrinal differences. I believe that if we are truly in pursuit of the truth and not establishing our revelations of God as truth, then there will be no need for discord. This was what the leaders of the early Church did in Acts 15 when there was discord about the doctrine that should be preached to the Gentile Christians.

I am praying that the Church will be united under the Lordship of Jesus Christ around the seat of truth so that we can arise to oppose the activities of Satan on the Earth. It is also important to note that God will severely punish all the Church leaders who have contributed to the discord of the Church, and this punishment shall happen suddenly, without any prior warning because they have misappropriated their authority and have misled the Church because of their personal gain:

> *But suppose that servant is wicked and says to himself, 'My master is staying away a long time', and he then begins to beat his fellow servants and to eat and drink with drunkards. The master of that servant will come on a day when he does not expect him and at an hour he is not aware of. He will cut him to pieces and assign him a place with the hypocrites, where there will be weeping and gnashing of teeth.* (Matthew 24:48–51 NIV)

The good news is that we don't need the entire Church to agree for us to exercise our authority and make great power available to withstand Satan. Jesus tells us that if two or three shall agree, it will be established. However, the influence of this group may be limited to the individual jurisdiction that makes up the group. Their agreement may not be powerful enough to affect the whole Earth. I will explain this further later on in this chapter.

The Limitation of the Church

The Church has the authority to do anything on the Earth. However, we do not have the authority to influence activities in the Heavens by decrees. Heavenly activities are outside our jurisdiction:

> *The Heaven, even the Heavens, are the* LORD'S*;*
> *But the Earth He has given to the children of men.*
> (Psalm 115:16 NKJV)

Therefore, if Heavenly activities are affecting the Earth, we cannot resist these activities by decreeing them away; we can only petition God to change them. The reason is that most Heavenly activities—both godly and demonic—are preordained in the Heavenly calendar to fulfil the will of God. Certain events take place on the Earth, which look ordinary to the human eye, but they are divinely orchestrated by God to bring the Kingdom of God on the Earth. However, we cannot always identify these activities except when they are revealed to us by the Holy Spirit. This is why sometimes Christians gather together to pray and nothing happens. It is because we are praying without the insight of the Holy Spirit.

Therefore, the Church cannot exercise authority on the Earth without the partnership of the Holy Spirit. It is for this reason that Jesus told the disciples to wait until the arrival of the Holy Spirit and they are endowed with power from on high (Acts 1: 4–8).

This is another area where Satan has opposed the Church. He has been very successful in influencing the Church to engage in worldly pursuits and becoming more administrative than spiritual. As a result, we are less yielding to the leading of the Holy Spirit and are focusing on principles that worldly organisations have used to become successful. We do not realise that we are exchanging our authority for worldly success. This is exactly what Esau did when he exchanged his birth right for a bowl of soup. We are forgoing the greater for the lesser. If we study the early Church, we discover that they were very successful because they were yielding to the Lordship of the Holy Spirit. As a result, great signs followed them, and they were able to exact influence on the affairs of the world.

The leadership of the Church needs to take responsibility for this. Jesus established a fivefold ministry structure (apostles, prophets, evangelists, pastors and teachers) to equip the Body of Christ for the work of the ministry and to bring us to maturity, with Him as the benchmark. After Peter and John were persecuted by the Sanhedrin for preaching Jesus at the temple in Acts 3 and 4, they (as leaders) gathered the Church to pray. The whole Church was filled with the Holy Spirit and spoke the Word of God with boldness. The problem with the Church is that most Church leaders are not building the Kingdom of God, but rather an empire fuelled by personal ambition. It is important to realise that this is exactly what Lucifer did, and this was the iniquity that was found in his heart. The result, as you know, was that he was cast out of God's Heaven. In many ways, most ministers have left the presence of God and are simply operating by human wisdom, a wisdom that came as a result of Adam's disobedience to God. This is why the Church is losing her influence and is now being influenced by the world. How can we then intercede when we too are enslaved to the same power that we should be delivering the world from? If we are to be effective in exercising our authority on the Earth, we must return to the Lordship of the Holy Spirit on the platform of the Word of God. If we do not pray by the Holy Spirit and following the scripture, our prayers will be without effect.

Another area of limitation is where a Satanic activity is occurring in partnership with the agency of man. As I mentioned before, God or Satan cannot do anything on the Earth, except by the agency of man. History shows that when God or the Devil wants to impact the Earth, they always partner with a human being. This is why God called Abraham, and why He worked through the prophets and the Church that rose after the ascension of Jesus Christ. God has willed the Earth to humanity, as depicted in Psalm 115:16. Therefore, He cannot go against His word by intervening in the affairs of men without the partnership of man.

It is for this reason that Jesus had to come in human form to deliver humanity from the power of sin and Satan. However, Satan had an unrestricted influence on man because he was able to subdue Adam and take his place as the Lord of the Earth. This is why Jesus, before His death, referred to Satan as the prince of this world. The world belonged to him because he took Adam's birthright until Jesus defeated him on the cross and rose again from the dead.

However, Satan remains the god of this world because he still has a majority of humanity—including some Christians—under his influence, which gives him license to lord over the Earth, although illegally.

The Church is limited by this because one human

being cannot overrule the will of another unless the human volunteers his will to the other. This, therefore, means that the Church cannot bind or control a human being through prayer. What we can do, instead, is release angelic activities through prayer to make it possible for humans under Satanic influences to hear God's Word and repent or receive the judgement of God.

An example is Pharaoh, the king of Egypt. Under Satanic influences, Pharaoh held the children of Israel captive for many years. God heard the cry of the children of Israel and worked signs and wonders in partnership with Moses as a witness to Pharaoh to release them. However, Pharaoh refused, and the result was God's judgement on him and Egypt. Please note that in the last plague, which resulted in the release of the children of Israel, God told Moses that He was passing judgement on all the gods of Egypt. This is a very important statement and reveals the real enemy at play.

Another example is Herod, who killed the Apostle James and arrested Peter with the same intention. But this time, the Church was praying. An angel of God was released as a result of the prayers of the Church to set Peter free and save him from the power of Herod. However, that was not the end of the angelic activity. God arranged an occasion for Herod to equate himself to God, and as a result, God's judgement was passed against him, and an angel of God struck him dead. He so died that his body decomposed instantly. In the same vein, the Body of Christ needs to pray for angelic activities, to either minister to the people that have opened themselves to Satanic influences, or bring judgement on them if they refuse to change. Nevertheless, the corporate prayers of the Church are only as potent as the prayers of the individual Christian.

Chapter 5

THE PRAYER OF THE INDIVIDUAL CHRISTIAN

The effective, fervent prayer of a righteous man avails much. (James 5:16 NKJV)

The prayers of the collective Church are only as powerful as the individuals that make up the collective. By this I mean, if the individuals who have come together to pray do not know what prayer is, or are not aware of their responsibility and authority, they will most likely not be in agreement, and their prayers may be ineffective. This is why each Christian needs to be taught about the authority he or she has in Christ Jesus and the resulting responsibility. Sadly, some of the people God has committed this responsibility to are only interested in building an empire for themselves; making themselves a mini-god to their congregation.

In Rick Joyner's book, *The Final Quest*, he recounts a vision he had about certain types of Christian groups in an army formation:

- The first group were fully furnished with weapons and the right armour.
- The second group had some armour and short swords, but their leaders were fully equipped.

- The third group did not have any amour, but their leaders were fully equipped.

The first group of Christians Rick Joyner saw are Christians who have been taught by their leaders to know their authority and how to use it. They have been brought up by the Word and Spirit of God and are equipped for the work of the ministry. These are the champions of God that, after they have heard a sermon on Sunday, go and corroborate and deepen the insight they have received in the place of prayer and their personal devotion. From this they get God's Word to them, which is called Rhema (the personalised revelation of God's Word), and they take this Rhema to impact their lives and the world. They are the true world changers.

The second group are Christians who have limited knowledge of the Word of God. They understand their place in the work of the ministry, but are still heavily dependent on the anointing of their pastor. They live and are motivated only by the words of their pastor and do not have a deep personal relationship with God. God's Word has not become real to them and their faith is based on the revelation of their pastor.

The third group are holiday Christians. Though they too, are committed, devout, God-fearing people, they do not even have the concept that God can speak to them, or that they themselves are workers in God's vineyard. They feel it is the job of others, and their faith is between them, God and their Church. They are not living for God but are interested in what God will do for them through the pastor or the Church they attend. These are the ones that are always looking for a miracle from one Church to the other. They are soldiers living the life of civilians—a life of illusions. It makes me so sad that some ministers are also this way.

God's Vision for the Christian

It is the vision and plan of God for every Christian to have a deep and personal connection with Him. God intended this from the beginning. Even during the time of Moses, God wanted each Israelite to have access to Him, but His presence frightened them. They told Moses to stand in their place and hear God for them. Please understand that this was why the ten commandments were given and why the Aaronic priesthood was constituted (Exodus 19-20). God never intended for us to live by a set of rules, but to live by relationship; to have a sense of right and wrong by proxy. Think about it. How did Joseph know it was wrong to sleep with Potiphar's wife? There were no commandments against this; neither was there any indication that the laws of the land prohibited it. Potiphar was only able to imprison Joseph because of his position in the Egyptian army. He probably would not have been able to do so as an ordinary civilian—who knows. What we do know, however, is that Joseph chose not to, because he feared God and respected his master. This is the product of relationship and a shadow of what the Christian life should look like. God's call to the Christian is a call to relationship—not religion. This relationship, like any other, only grows with consistent communication, which is expressed in the place of personal devotion and constant prayer.

It is the vision of God for us to come boldly to His throne of grace. This is why the first thing that happened at the death of Jesus is the tearing of the temple veil—the opening up of the Holy of Holies—to mark the end of the Aaronic priesthood and the need for some men to represent others to God. We now all have access, as many as desire, to enter. Therefore, we should not act like the babes of the Old Testament, who were waiting for someone to prophesy to them before they heard God's Word. God wants you to hear Him for yourself in the place of prayer. The office of a prophet to the individual Christian is not to tell you what God is saying, but to teach you how to hear from God and confirm what God is already telling you. Prophets who have been well trained do not prophesy to those maturing in Christ; they have a light in their spirit that God is already talking to or dealing with that person, about a particular subject. The words of a prophet are the primary source of divine direction for those who are losing their way and those who cannot yet discern God's voice for themselves.

Prayer is a place of encounter for the Christian and a place of answers. It is also a place where we exercise our authority and make change happen. In the opening scripture for this chapter, we see James admonishing the Christians across the world that the effectual and persistent prayer of the righteous avails much power. That means it is not until we commit ourselves to a continuous and consistent prayer lifestyle that we make the power available to affect change in the world. I believe that the reason the world is heading where it is today is because Christians are not praying, but are distracted by the pursuit of the good things in life. Satan has successfully deceived and distracted us by sending us on a fool's errand after the riches of this world, while he controls the affairs of the world. The things we are chasing are ours anyway, and he knows it. But as long as he can continue to deceive us to see riches (which God gave us as tools) as destinations, we will not be able to take our place as the gods of the Earth, and Satan will continue his illegal reign and operations. Please note that this is not the plan of God for the world today. Therefore, as Christians, we need to have a strong prayer life. By this, I don't necessarily mean our supplications alone, but prayer as a platform to hear from God, which will help us focus on the things that matter most.

Distractions are one of Satan's biggest weapons against the Christian. As Children of God and joint heirs with Christ, Satan does not have any power over us. He can only distract us from seeing our authority and talk us out of our heritage, just as he did with Adam and Eve. In every attack of the enemy, whether it be to your finances, marriage, family or your health, the focus is to get your eyes off God and your true identity. Only after he has done this has he gained mastery over you. Our call is to stand firm in the place of prayer and resist the devil by focusing on the Word of God and being led by the Spirit. If you feel attacked by the enemy, you need to stand still and rest in God so that you can do the work that God has called you to do, regardless of your circumstances. Don't let Satan trap you by making you wallow in your circumstances. Rise as the Child of God that you are. Put the Word of God in your mouth and prophesy it over that situation today!

The Authority of the Individual Christian

Every Christian has authority. Jesus said that He has given us authority over all the abilities of the Devil (Luke 10:19). He also said that certain signs will follow those who believe in His name:

1. They will speak in new tongues.
2. They will cast out demons.
3. They will lay their hands on the sick and they will recover.
4. Nothing shall by any means hurt them (Mark 16:17).

The above are signs, proving that we believe and are disciples of Jesus Christ. These signs are available to every Christian—not just ministers of God. Therefore, every Christian has been given authority over all the abilities of the enemy. Jesus was not just talking to the disciples of that day. He was also talking to you and me today. We have authority over all the abilities of the enemy! All means, excluding nothing. This means that there is nothing Satan can do that you and I do not already have the authority to disarm. So you can deal with the activities of Satan in your life, home, community and your world. You can have an effect anywhere if you trust in what the Word of God says over you. However, the tool by which we exercise this influence is prayer. When you pray, believing that you will receive what have asked for, you will have it (Mark 11:24). This is a law of faith set in place by our Lord Jesus Christ. Therefore, as Christians, we are responsible for exercising God's authority over our lives and our world through prayer. Whatever you need to change in your life or your world, you can change through prayer.

Consider the life of Elijah. When he was introduced in 1 Kings 17, he was not a prophet, but as a man who confronted an evil King of Israel. It was after this action we knew Elijah as a prophet. What I am saying here, is that you do not need to get a call to ministry before you take on the responsibility of prayer. In some cases, the mantle of ministry may not be released until you are first giving to prayer. Having said that, the call of ministry usually starts with a burden of prayer.

I remember when God was calling me into evangelical ministry and apostolic ministry to young people.

This call started with a burden to pray for souls who did not know God and to intercede for young people in London. It did not start with me just preaching alone, but with the burden to pray. It is in the place of prayer that the door of ministry opens and grace is given to operate in the office you are called into. We will discuss more on this in the next chapter. The point here is that as a Christian, you can take control of your life, household, community and your world through prayer. You can realign every activity that is outside the will and purpose of God, in any area of your life, back into the will of God through prayer. You don't need anyone to do the praying for you. You can do it yourself.

Imagine if every Christian knew this and acted on it. Think about the change we would make in the world. This brings to mind the statement Joshua made: that one shall chase a thousand and two shall put ten thousand to flight (Joshua 23:10). If one person's prayer life can affect a thousand people, and two, ten thousand, imagine what we all can do if we strengthen our individual prayer lives and pray in unity with our brothers and sisters in Christ. We can change the world and exercise the will of God on the Earth. Therefore, arise and pray!

Chapter 6

MINISTRY AND PRAYER

> *Therefore, I exhort first of all that supplications, prayers, intercessions, and giving of thanks be made for all men, for kings and all who are in authority, that we may lead a quiet and peaceable life in godliness and reverence.*
> (1 Timothy 2:1–2 NKJV)

Every Christian has been called into a ministry. The Bible teaches that there are good works that God planned for us to do before the foundation of the world (Ephesians 2:10). These works are ministerial. Paul explains that we are members of the Body of Christ, His actual body on the Earth (Ephesians 5:30). Each one of us has a part to play in the body. He further explains in his letter to the Romans:

> *For as we have many members in one body, but all the members do not have the same function, so we, being many, are one body in Christ, and individually members of one another. Having then gifts differing according to the grace that is given to us, let us use them: if prophecy, let us prophesy in proportion to our faith; or ministry, let us use it in our ministering; he who teaches, in teaching; he*

> *who exhorts, in exhortation; he who gives, with liberality; he who leads, with diligence; he who shows mercy, with cheerfulness.* (Romans 12:4–8 NKJV)

Some of us may be called to teach; some may be given the ministry of hospitality, music or administration, and so on. The key thing is that we all identify what our part is in the body and play it faithfully. Having said this, we all have been called to the ministry of reconciliation—that is, winning souls for God. This assignment is our primary calling. Therefore, it doesn't matter what else you are doing for God; if you have not made yourself available to God as a soul winner, then you are already outside of God's will for your life. However, we cannot be effective in soul winning or any activity that will result in the advancement of God's Kingdom, if we are not first effective in the place of prayer. It is a praying Christian, who is sound in the Word of God and led by the Holy Spirit, that will be a winner and fruitful in God's vineyard.

In Chapter 3 we discussed that our enemy is not flesh and blood but the Satanic echelon. We have reviewed their ranks and responsibilities as assigned by their supreme leader, Satan. At this point, we need to know that the spirit responsible for keeping the Gospel of Jesus Christ from reaching the heart of unbelievers is no one other than Satan himself. He does not delegate this task to any other spirit (2 Corinthians 4:4). Therefore, the main call of the Christian is being resisted at the top of the Satanic hierarchy. Is there any wonder why we always face severe opposition when preaching the Gospel? This is why prayer is important.

When I did street evangelism in West London some years ago, I spent a considerable amount of time praying before and after each trip. The reason I prayed even before I walked out of the house to preach was that I was already facing resistance from within—thoughts discouraging me not to go, coupled with the memories of cold responses from those I had summoned the courage to speak with about the Lord Jesus Christ. It was very hard, I must admit. This is why we need to pray. Jesus tells us that until you bind a strong man, you cannot go in to despoil his house. Every unbeliever is of Satan's household. Do you think he will let you enter his house to take those he has held in captivity without a fight? Of course not. He will do everything he can, not only to stop you from entering, but to ensure that *you* become one of his captives again—for we were all once a captive of Satan. Therefore, true evangelism starts with prayer because it is in the place of prayer that we destroy the stronghold of Satan that stops people from believing the Gospel. Until that stronghold is destroyed, they cannot believe, even if they want to. Therefore, without effective prayer, evangelism will just be another fruitless religious activity.

Breakthrough in Prayer

I recently heard a man give testimony about his association with witchcraft and the occult. He mentioned how he partnered with fallen angels and demons to attack people and Churches. What struck me about his testimony was that he mentioned there is a thick black cloud over regions where people do not fear God, closing them off from Heaven. He mentioned that this cloud is designed to obstruct prayers from ascending to Heaven and receiving answers. According to his testimony, there are three levels of Christian prayer:

1. The faint prayer
2. The intermediate prayer
3. The fervent prayer

When a Christian, especially a Christian that has been previously distracted, starts praying, their prayers start as a faint prayer. It looks like a very faint smoke that does not even rise to reach the thick cloud. However, as they persist in prayer, the smoke gets thicker and gathers momentum, moving to the intermediate prayer. It is at this point that the Christian becomes a threat and demonic forces are sent to dissuade them from prayer. This is why we get distracted as we pray or even get a fake sense of victory over our difficulties to dissuade us from praying. If the enemy can dissuade the Christian, his prayer will not have gained enough momentum to break through the thick cloud over that region. But if the Christian can continue, then the smoke becomes a volcanic fire that cannot be stopped by any force, rising directly into Heaven. The man testifying stated that every prayer that breaks through the cloud always receive answers. Not only that, but the hole created means that the Christian will operate under an open Heaven, making the Christian a super target for demonic forces.

This revelation shows why we must be diligent in the place of prayer and not relent. We do not pray fervently to convince God to answer our prayer. We pray fervently so that our prayers break through the Satanic opposition and rise to Heaven. This is what the concept of 'breakthrough' means. However, more than this, I believe God does not just want us to have personal breakthroughs in prayer, He wants us to destroy the cloud altogether.

The call of the Christian is to restore the desolate heritages. As previously mentioned, every Christian can gain authority over regions through faithfulness in prayer. As we pray for the regions we live in, we can destroy every demonic influence and the thick cloud over that region, ensuring that the region is operating under open Heavens. We can also request godly angels to take charge of those regions. When we do this, we make it easier for people living in those places to encounter God and experience favour in their lives. The more we do this, the more we weaken the global Satanic influence.

Prayer releases angelic activities on the Earth. When a prayer goes up to Heaven, an angel is sent with the answer to the prayer. However, the angel can be attacked and arrested by fallen angels ruling over those regions. We see this in the story of Daniel when, after Daniel had prayed, the angel Gabriel was released with the answer to Daniel's prayer. However, he was arrested by the prince of Persia and held with the kings of Persia—demonic forces responsible for the activities in the regions over which Persia ruled. Gabriel was not released until Michael came down to assist him. Please note that Michael did not come down until Daniel continued in prayer. This is why a lot of prayers are not answered. When we pray and do not receive answers immediately, we often give up hope. But we see from the life of Daniel that when we pray, God hears us and releases immediate answers. However, the angels who have been sent with these answers are usually opposed by Satanic forces, stopping our prayers from reaching us. Sometimes these prayers are stolen and given to occultist forces. When people consult occultic agents as a medium to solve their problems, these stolen prayers are the gifts that these agents give them. Therefore, anything you receive from the devil was stolen from someone else—or perhaps, even from you. However, we can break these Satanic interceptions by being persistent and fervent in the place of prayer, just as Daniel was.

Prayer of Intercession

The prayer of Daniel was both a prayer of intercession, because he was standing in the gap for the nation of Judah, and a legal plea to God, based on what he had read in the books written by the prophet Jeremiah about the number of years Judah would be in captivity in Babylon. That number was already completed, but God had not yet performed His Word. The reason Daniel needed to intercede was that the Jews were still living in sin, inconsistent with God's covenant, and so it became inconsistent with the nature of God to bless them.

Therefore, Daniel needed to make a legal argument based on the Word of God to make it consistent with God to deliver the Jews from Babylon and restore them to the Promised Land. The example of Daniel shows that a nation is delivered by the prayer of the saints in, associated with, or called to the nation.

Until we pray, God cannot do anything. I say this emphatically because God has given us the Earth and He will not violate His covenant by intervening in the Earth without an invitation from the man that He has given it to. Intercession is even more important when citizens of the nation have wilfully given their lives over to Satan, either by acts of continuous sin and wickedness to their fellow man, or by direct association with Satan through worship—idolatry, association with fraternities and the occult. Such a nation has willingly made Satan their god, and it is this type of nation that is closed to Heaven by the thick cloud we discussed earlier. Therefore, a legal plea, or prayer of intercession, needs to be made to God to break the Satanic influence over that nation. Until this is done, it is impossible to have any serious impact on God's kingdom in that nation. At best, you will be able to empower the Christians to break through the thick cloud and receive answers from God for themselves. However, that nation will still be under Satanic rule, and it won't be long before that nation takes out their frustration on the Church and persecutes its members.

It is for this reason that we must be concerned about our nation. This is why Paul instructed Timothy:

> *Therefore, I exhort first of all that supplications, prayers, intercessions, and giving of thanks be made for all men, for kings and all who are in authority, that we may lead a quiet and peaceable life in all godliness and reverence.* (1 Timothy 2:1–2 NKJV)

We cannot lead a peaceable life if the nation is in darkness. Remember that Daniel was at the highest level of government in Babylon—under both the Babylonian and Persian Empires. He was probably doing better in Babylon than he did in Judah. Therefore, Daniel may not have had a personal advantage in returning to Judah, because he was comfortable where he was. However, he still prayed for the deliverance of his nation even if it came at the expense of his comfort. It is a shame that most Christians are not like Daniel. We have faith for God to move in our lives, but we do not care about what happens in the life of our neighbour, and even less in our nation. Although Daniel is very junior to us in the Kingdom of God, because he does not have the Holy Spirit in the same measure in which we do, he did a lot with very little. Are we doing little to nothing even though God dwells in us in His fullness?

We need to pray for our nation. If we don't, the work of God will continue to face aggressive opposition because we will not be pushing back the forces against us. Please note that many Churches will be closed down and evangelism frustrated if we do not pray. Oh! It is so important that we pray. If we don't, Satan will be able to carry out his activities unhindered. This will lead to the destruction of many nations. Satan is the one that weakens nations and brings them to poverty and destruction (Isaiah 14:12). He has succeeded in doing this for so long because the Church has been sleeping. There is no other force that can oppose Satan, except Jesus. But Jesus resides in His Body—the Church. If the Body is not active, how can the Person be active? Jesus needs us to pray so that His will can be exacted on the Earth. Again, if we do not pray, this will not happen.

I know some people reading this book may think to themselves, 'But we raise prayer points for our nation at Church'. I am not talking about praying religious prayers at Church, but praying for your nation with a sense of assignment, just as you would pray when you are facing personal tribulations and challenges. I am asking you to pray as if you are praying to be delivered from death. Pray as if your life depends on it. Pray from the groaning of your heart. Pray as Daniel prayed.

We need to rid ourselves of the individualism in Christianity. The only form of individualism in Christianity is the decision to become a Christian and to remain a Christian. Those are the only two things you need to be selfish about. Everything else has to do with the Body and the nation to which you have been sent to, or operate in.

A lot of Christians are not prospering because they are only thinking about their welfare. If you study the lives of the people that God prospered, you will discover that God prospered them because of their nations—not because of themselves or their family. When God wants to prosper a man or woman, he looks for someone who has a heart for the nation and tests them in the place of service. The minute you lose interest in your nation, you limit the scope of God's grace and, consequently, His blessing on your life. This is why the Bible says that those who seek the prosperity of Zion shall prosper.

If you share the same passions as God, He will use you beyond what you can imagine. God is passionate for all to be saved. He is also passionate for the restoration of the desolate heritages—the nations that are under the control of Satanic rebel forces. You cannot be a success in ministry, or life, if you are not praying for your nation. True ministry starts on your knees.

Every great revival was born out of the place of fervent prayer. The Welsh revival started from a small group of Christians praying. Pastor David Yonggi Cho was only able to build the biggest congregation the modern world has seen because of prayer. Any victory that we see, on the pulpit or publicly, was first won in the place of prayer. Jesus confirmed this to His disciples when He told them there are demons that do not go except by prayer and fasting.

Therefore, we must be fervent in prayer for our nation, the world and the lost souls. As we press in prayer, we make power available to prophesy God's will on the Earth and hidden secrets to be made known to us, just as we read in the lives of Elijah and Daniel.

Chapter 7

PROPHECY AND PRAYER

But earnestly desire the best gifts.
And yet I show you a more excellent way.
(1 Corinthians 12:31 NKJV)

When I was a leader at the Christian Union in my college many years ago, I was jealous of one of the other leaders who always seemed to prophesy to other people. So I took my feelings to God in prayer and discussed my desire to prophesy to others. God's response was, 'How many people do you pray for?' This, of course, left me dumbfounded. He then explained that intercession was the secret to prophesy and the secret to intercession is to walk in love. To validate this word with scripture, let's consider three people who I believe exemplify what God told me.

Moses

Moses was an adopted prince of Egypt who could not contain his love for his people. The Bible tells us that Moses refused to be called the son of Pharaoh's daughter and subjected himself to the same suffering as his fellow Hebrew brothers and sisters (Hebrews 11:24). His love for the Hebrews was so deep that he killed an Egyptian who was maltreating a Hebrew. This incident however, led to his exile from Egypt, where he spent forty years shepherding his father-in-law's sheep, until God called him to become the deliverer of Israel. I believe it was the love that Moses had for God's people that qualified him for the next forty years of his life.

During Moses' first encounter with Pharaoh, he requested that Pharaoh release the children of Israel from the land of Egypt. Instead, Pharaoh increased the workload of the children of Israel as a punishment for Moses' audacity. This drove Moses to cry out to God, which led to the ten plagues of Egypt and the eventual exodus of Israel to the Red Sea, where God delivered them completely from the grasp of Pharaoh through Moses and set them on course for the Promised Land.

During the wilderness journey, the children of Israel complained of either thirst or hunger, and each time, Moses took their complaints to God in prayer and received the direction to provide for their needs. The people experienced God's miracles throughout their journey because Moses was interceding for them. It got to a point when God was tired of the children of Israel's requests and wanted to destroy them and raise a new nation from the seed of Moses. But Moses interceded for them before God and was able to stop God's wrath from wiping out Israel.

Deborah

Deborah was one of the judges of Israel. She was known as a prophetess and was referred to as a Mother in Israel. Many came to her for counsel and judgement. It was clear that she loved the people. At this time, the children of Israel had sinned against God, and, as a result, He allowed the King of Canaan to subjugate them. When the time of deliverance came, God commanded Deborah to instruct Barak to take ten thousand soldiers to fight against the Canaanite army. In Hebrew culture, women didn't give orders. According to Levitical laws, they did not even have an inheritance because they would be married into another family. However, Deborah was distinguished in that, although she was the wife of Lapidoth, she was still able to command a man to lead an army against enemy forces. The simple obedience from the man she commanded is, in itself an act of God, but what is even more striking is that Barak was only willing to go if Deborah followed him, even at the expense of losing the glory of winning the battle to a woman. What did Barak know that made him humble himself to a woman in this way, even though it was against their culture to do so?

The Bible tells us that the Canaanite army had nine hundred chariots of iron, which signified a formidable military force. These weapons were what they used to oppress the Israelites. The Bible also tells us that there was no shield or spear found amongst forty thousand men in Israel. So Israel did not have a long-range attack strategy, and neither did they have any means of defence. Therefore, Barak knew that they could not depend on military might to conquer the Canaanite army. They needed something that only Deborah might be able to help them with—God's intervention.

On the battlefield, when the enemy forces approached, Barak arose to attack at Deborah's command. The next thing we saw was that God routed the chariots of Canaan, indicating that God disarmed their military weapons. As a result, it stopped being a battle and became a pursuit and a massacre. None of the Canaanite soldiers survived. I believe that this victory was possible because as Barak was fighting, Deborah was praying. I believe it was her prayer that won the battle, not the army of Israel.

Elijah

Elijah was a battle axe in God's hands against Ahab and Jezebel because of the wickedness they had caused in Israel. His first appearance is in 1 King 17 when he walked into the palace of Ahab and announced that there would not be rain for three and a half years. Please note that he did not say that *God said* there wouldn't be rain. Elijah was the one who said there would not be rain. His words shut the Heavens for more than three years. In the book of James, we have a clearer understanding of what happened:

> *Elijah was a man with a nature like ours, and he prayed earnestly that it would not rain; and it did not rain on the land for three years and six months. And he prayed again, and the Heaven gave rain, and the Earth produced its fruit.* (James 5: 17–18 NKJV)

Elijah prayed earnestly that it would not rain to force the children of Israel back to repentance.

We see Elijah in the house of the widow of Zarephath when she lost her son. Elijah prayed and brought the child back to life. We see when he challenged the prophets of Baal to call their god to receive their sacrifice by sending fire from Heaven. Baal did not answer. But when Elijah prayed, God answered by fire. We also see Elijah after the three and a half years when he prayed again, and there was rain. The prayer and prophecy of Elijah was born from the place of love and a strong desire to see the children of Israel return to the God of Israel.

Prayer Breeds Prophecy

As we can see from the examples of Moses, Deborah and Elijah, prophecy comes out of the place of prayer. As we become committed to praying for our nation, God will open our eyes to hidden mysteries and give us the words of prophecy to declare. It is these words of prophecy that will bring change, just as they did in the days of Moses, Deborah and Elijah.

Moses had to declare the judgement over Egypt for it to happen.

Deborah had to declare the time of God's deliverance before the children of Israel could be set free from the bondage of Canaan.

Elijah had to declare that there wouldn't be rain before the Heavens were shut.

In the same vein, we need to declare what God is saying for it to happen. But as the three prophets received these words of prophecy in the place of prayer, we must also receive words of prophecy in prayer.

A Call to Intercession

After the Jews were taken as captives to Babylon, God told Ezekiel that He looked for a man to stand in the gap so that He would not punish Judah, but He couldn't find one (Ezekiel 22:30). The Bible tells us that the eye of the Lord searches the Earth to find people who will trust Him enough to allow Him to demonstrate His power through them (2 Chronicles 16:9). God is looking for people who will cry out for their nation. He is looking for people through whom He will demonstrate His power. But how can God still be looking when the Body of Christ is on the Earth? We need to wake up and start interceding. I am not talking about the disingenuous prayers we have been praying. We need to pray with the heart that Moses, Deborah, Elijah and Daniel had. Deborah said in her song, 'My heart is with the rulers of Israel who offered themselves willingly with the people. Bless the Lord!' (Judges 5:9 NKJV)

Where is your heart? Is it with your pocket or for the deliverance and prosperity of your nation? God is looking for a people that will arise with their nation in their heart and call down His will on the Earth. If we do not do this, wickedness will continue to reign on the Earth, and Satan will continue his destructive operations unhindered. Again, I say with tears in my heart, it is time for us to pray as if our lives depend on it—because they just might. Only then will we see God move upon the Earth as prophesied long ago.

Chapter 8

REVIVAL AND PRAYER

Ask the LORD for rain in the time of the latter rain. The LORD will make flashing clouds; He will give them showers of rain, grass in the field for everyone. (Zechariah 10:1 NKJV)

Revivals are ushered in by prayer. The Bible says when the cloud is full of rain, they will empty themselves on the Earth (Ecclesiastes 11:3). When we press in the place of prayer, we saturate the atmosphere, and before long, the rain of revival will begin to pour. We need to understand that every move of God recorded in history was a product of prayer. Whenever God wants to move on the Earth, He raises a man to pray His will down, either by intercession, prophesy, acts of faith or confessions. This is why God raised prophets and judges in the Old Testament. They served as conduits to bring His will on the Earth.

God raised Abraham because God wanted to consecrate his lineage to bring the Messiah to the world and to serve as an example of the faithful lifestyle required for salvation. God took Abraham on this journey of faith so that his acts of obedience would serve as an intercession to bring the will of God on the Earth. Abraham became a living intercession, a witness before

God to save mankind from Satan's bondage and the power of sin and death. This is why I believe that God told Abraham that through him all the nations of the Earth would be blessed.

Consider these questions:

- Why did Abraham have to wait for Isaac?
- Why was it important that Abraham believed God's Word?
- What was the essence of the covenant of circumcision?
- Why did God instruct Abraham to sacrifice Isaac even though he waited twenty-five years for him?
- Why did God not consider the other children of Abraham, but only focused on Isaac?

Abraham had to wait on God and believe Him even before he saw the physical manifestation of what he longed for. He needed to learn to depend on God's Word more than his perceived reality and teach his seed to do the same. God's Word needed to be his sole source of reality. This is why the Bible tells us that Abraham did not consider the deadness of his own body. That means that he only considered the Word of God. In the same vein, when we give our lives to Christ, we no longer consider the corruption of our Earthly body nor the sinful nature that we inherited from Adam, we now only consider the life of Christ we have by faith in God's Word. Like Abraham, we have lifted the immaterial above the material; the invisible above the visible. It is no wonder the Bible teaches that it is those who are of the faith of Abraham that will inherit the promise of salvation and are considered the children of Abraham (Romans 4:16; Galatians 3:7). Therefore, to become engrafted into the Commonwealth of Israel and partake in the free gift of salvation, we have to believe in the same way Abraham believed.

God commanded Abraham to sacrifice Isaac to create a witness to the obedience of his faith. If Abraham could be obedient enough to sacrifice the son of promise that he loved so much, just because God commanded him to do so, then God too could sacrifice His only Son, the One He loves—for the sake of mankind. A closer look at the following scriptures will help bring this point home:

> *Then He said, 'Take now your son,* ***your only son*** Isaac, ***whom you love****, and go to the land of Moriah, and offer him there as a burnt offering on one of the mountains of which I shall tell you'.* (Genesis 22:2 NKJV)

> *For God so loved the world that He gave His* ***only begotten Son****, that whoever believes in Him should not perish but have everlasting life ...****The Father loves the Son****, and has given all things into His hand.* (John 3:16; 35 NKJV)

The following facts and comparison can be drawn out from these scriptures:

- Abraham was instructed to sacrifice Isaac, the only son birthed by his wife Sarah.
- God sacrificed Jesus, His only begotten Son.
- Abraham loved Isaac.
- God loved Jesus.

Therefore, the command God gave to Abraham was directly proportionate to the sacrifice God made. Another interesting fact is that Mount Moriah, the place where God commanded Abraham to sacrifice Isaac, is the same place as Golgotha, the place where Jesus was crucified. Abraham's act of obedience was a direct demonstration of God's heart and intention. When Abraham took that step of faith to obey God, God's intention to sacrifice Jesus was sealed. That is why the Angel of Lord immediately appeared to stop Abraham and a ram was provided as a substitute for Isaac. The ram represents Jesus (a full-grown son), who was to be sacrificed on the very same spot.

The example of Abraham demonstrates that intercession is not just about saying words of prayer—even though that is important—but about leading a life of obedience in agreement with God's Word. This is a more powerful witness before God than any prayer we can say to Him. In fact, our prayers of will be more effective if we are leading a life of obedience to God's word.

The Principle of the Remnant

The covenant of circumcision was given because God wanted to raise a remnant for Himself on the Earth who would be His people. Those who were circumcised carried the confirmation of God's covenant with Abraham, showing that they had been separated from the world unto God. From generation to generation, the covenant of circumcision continued from Abraham to Isaac, then to Jacob and then to the nation of Israel. Therefore, the nation of Israel became a memorial to God, reminding Him of His covenant with Abraham. He indicated that through him the world would be blessed and saved through his lineage. As a result, Israel became an intercession before God, reminding Him of His covenant to save mankind from sin. Whenever God wants to do something on the Earth, He raises a remnant that will stand before Him.

To drive this point home, let us once again consider the life Abraham. In Genesis 18, we see God appearing to Abraham with two angels to reaffirm the promise of Isaac to Abraham. When He was about to leave, God revealed to Abraham His intention to destroy Sodom and Gomorrah, because He knew that Abraham would teach his generations. But Abraham knew the principle of God and upon that principle, he interceded for Sodom and Gomorrah, because of his nephew, Lot. So, he said to God, 'If You find a remnant who are righteous, will You still destroy the city with the righteous?'

God said that He wouldn't. In Genesis 19, the Bible shows us the depravity in Sodom and that God could not destroy Sodom and Gomorrah until Lot had left the city, because of Abraham.

The principle of the remnant continued throughout the lineage of Jacob. Every time the nation of Israel sinned, there was always a remnant who sought the face of God, and, in most cases, out of this remnant came a deliverer for Israel.

Jesus further emphasised the principle of the remnant when He gave this parable:

> *The kingdom of Heaven is like a merchant seeking beautiful pearls, who, when he had found one pearl of great price, went and sold all that he had and bought it.* (Matthew 13:45–46 NKJV)

In this parable, Jesus made it clear that the field was bought because of the pearl that he found, not because he felt the whole field was valuable. Therefore, the entire field belongs to him, because of the one pearl that he found. Why did Jesus use this analogy to describe the Kingdom of God? It is because that was what God did. God gave all that He had to save the world because of the remnant He had kept for Himself through the seed of Abraham—not just biologically, but also all who will be saved by the faith of Abraham.

God moves on the Earth because of His remnant. God's remnant today is the Church because we are the result of God's covenant with Abraham. We carry the spiritual circumcision, which is the Holy Spirit who has sealed us and is the evidence that we belong to God. Therefore, if there will be a change in this world, if there will be a revival, it will be because of the Church.

Changes don't come by revolutions or riots, they come because of the prayers of the saints. Only our prayers can bring lasting change to the world. Therefore, we need to rise and pray for the wind of change to blow in this world.

The world is getting darker and darker as we get closer to the rapture of the Church. However, before we leave the Earth, we need to ensure that God's will is enforced on the Earth. This is the true meaning of revival. It is not just about seeing miracles everywhere; it is not just about souls coming to Christ. It is about the enforcement of God's will over the nations so that Satan cannot carry out the destruction he intends before God's time. It is the job of the Church to stop him and stop him we must—but we can only do this through prayer.

Chapter 9

THE HOLY SPIRIT AND PRAYER

For the Spirit searches all things, yes, the deep things of God. (1 Corinthians 2:10)

There is no other time in the whole of history that it has been more important for Christians to be sensitive to the leading of the Holy Spirit, than the time we are living in now. It is God's desire for us to know His will and to walk in it. However, we cannot know His will solely with our minds. The Holy Spirit helps us discern the will of God. He is the One Who searches out the will of God and puts it in our hearts.

Often, Christians get involved in what seems to be a righteous or good cause and then discover that it is not as it seemed. This is why the Bible admonishes us that we should no longer know according to the flesh, but according to the Spirit (2 Corinthians 5:16). Let's consider Joshua when the Gibeonites deceived him and the children of Israel to make a covenant with them (Joshua 9). These people were disguised as foreigners from a distant land even though they were indigenous to the land of Canaan. They came to Joshua to ask for a covenant that he would not destroy them like the other nations. Joshua agreed, but the Bible tells us that they did not seek the Lord. After the children of Israel discovered the deceit, they could not go back on their word. This covenant had generational consequences, because hundreds of years later there was a famine in Israel to avenge the killings of the Gibeonites, which was led by King Saul. David had to sacrifice seven of Saul's sons upon the request of the Gibeonites to appease the anger of God. Think about it: How many partnerships, marriages, or business arrangements that we have entered have now become a snare that we cannot get out off?

This is why we need to pray and seek the face of God, not just for what we can get from Him, but to understand His will.

I believe that one of the reasons that Christians are ineffective is because we do not take enough time with the Holy Spirit to know the will of God; and just as with Joshua and the Israelite, we make decisions with our emotions and warped moral compass. We say to ourselves, 'If it feels right, then it must be right', and, as a result, we sometimes get ourselves in hot water and introduce battles into our lives that should have never existed—and only because we did not take time to know God's will for us.

> *But the Helper, the Holy Spirit, whom the Father will send in My name, He will teach you all things, and* ***bring to your remembrance all things that I said to you... He will guide you into all truth****; for*

> *He will not speak on His own authority,* but whatever He hears He will speak; ***and He will tell you things to come****. (John 14:26; 16:13 NKJV)*

According to scripture, the Holy Spirit reminds us of the past, gives us insight into the present and knowledge of the future. Think about the number of atrocities in the world that could have been prevented if we knew the future. Imagine if we had a foreknowledge of what Hitler would do to the Jews when he put them in isolation centres that became extermination centres. If the Jews and the entire international community knew that those were the plans of Hitler, surely they would have stopped him.

But how will we know for certain when those who have been given access to this knowledge are distracted by their desires? Jesus told us that the world cannot receive the Holy Spirit. Only Christians can. It is the job of the Church to know, declare, prepare and establish God's will on the Earth and stop the advancement of evil in the world.

God said to Jeremiah, 'Call unto Me, and I will show you great and mighty things'. (Jeremiah 33:3) These great and mighty things refer to knowledge that has been locked up and fenced in. No human discovery or research can uncover hidden realities that are released from God's throne. Unless He shows us, we cannot know. Do you remember what Elisha said when the son of the rich woman who took care of him died?

He said she seemed troubled, 'but God has not revealed it to me'. Elisha was a prophet, but he realised he could only know what God revealed to him. In the same way, we only know what God has revealed to us, and the Bible tells us that the righteous shall be delivered by knowledge (Proverbs 11:9).

An example of this is in Acts 11 when the prophet Agabus declared that there would be a famine throughout the Roman world. As a result of this information, the Christians could send relief to their brothers and sisters who would be affected by the famine ahead of time. Similarly, Joseph, because he could interpret the dream that God gave Pharaoh, was able to prepare for the famine to come and save the known world. Perhaps this was what made Egypt the most powerful nation of that time. We also learn from scripture that the sons of Issachar were chiefs in the land because they knew how to discern times and seasons (1 Chronicles 12:32).

Our ability to know is what makes us leaders. Look at the COVID-19 pandemic. Only God knows exactly what is going on behind the scenes. I wish I was sensitive enough to the Holy Spirit to have known how bad it would have been before it happened. The point here is that we as Christians should not be caught unaware by world events. We should know, declare, prepare and execute. Noah knew there was going to be a flood; Abraham knew that God would destroy Sodom and Gomorrah; Isaac was directed by God's wisdom to stay in Canaan, and he prospered despite the famine; Jacob prophesied the future of all of his twelve sons; Joseph knew that there would be a famine in Egypt, and when he was about to die, he knew that God would one day take the children of Israel out of Egypt. We can go on about Daniel, David and the rest of the prophets who understood the power of divine alignment with God's will. So why is the Church today ignorant? We need to be sensitive to the Holy Spirit, unless we too want to be deceived by the world.

Let us consider this: Why was the first horseman at the breaking of the first seal a white horse who went out with a bow? Considering that the other horsemen that followed were famine, death, Hades and war, why was the first one white? This is a message to the discerning mind. God was revealing the horrors that Satan will bring to the world in the last days after the Church has been raptured. It will first appear like something good, noble—a no-brainer (like the COVID-19 vaccines) only to reveal a malicious intention after. Why was someone with such a small stature—like Hitler—able to command such a large following? Why did people believe in his vision and rally around him? This is because his initial intentions seemed noble to the German nation who needed something to believe in after going through the horrors of the First World War.

Hitler was seen as their knight in shining armour who would revive the German might. If they knew Hitler's true intentions, would they still have supported him? Maybe not. We have seen the same thing repeated throughout history. The world arises to support a particular ideology only to discover the evil it was intended for when it is too late. This was what happened with slavery and colonialism. It is what is still happening today with some so-called foreign aid and foreign direct investments. They are presented to these nations as an opportunity for growth and development. However, I would argue that it is simply a ploy to steal their resources.

The question every Christian needs to be asking themselves today is: What ideologies are you currently supporting that you realise did not come from God and are evil in disguise? Did the Black Lives Matter movement come from God? Did the End SARS movement come from God? As seemingly noble and justifiable as these things may be, it remains to be seen if they were divinely orchestrated, or if they are just evil in disguise used to reinforce other agendas; like I believe the Pride movement to be. We as Christians, need to know what we are getting involved in unless we want to continue in the trap the world has fallen in.

Before we get ourselves into anything, we need to know what the will of God is and what His wisdom is for that situation. Until we know this, our prayers cannot truly be effective, because we will pray amiss. The Holy Spirit has been given to us by God the Father to help us with our prayers. The Bible tells us that we do not know how to pray as we ought, but the Holy Spirit intercedes for us with groaning that is too deep to utter.

Therefore, the best position a Christian can ever be in is to be yielded to the Holy Spirit. It is only Him that reveals the divine strategies God has put together for us to excel in this dark and evil world. Unless we are yielding to Him and set time aside to fellowship with Him, we will be like hidden lights blending into a dark and cruel world. It is time for us to listen, know, declare, prepare, execute—these things can only be done when we spend time with the Holy Spirit in the place of prayer.

Chapter 10

PRAYING THE RIGHT WAY

Therefore I say to you, whatever things you ask when you pray, believe that you receive them and you will have them.
(Mark 11:24 NKJV)

It is the mandate of every Christian to pray. However, Christians are not the only ones who pray. All religions have one form of prayer or another. Nevertheless, what makes us different is the attitude with which we pray.

Jesus told us that whatever we desire when we pray, we should believe we will receive and we shall have it. This therefore, indicates that God wants us to pray with an attitude of certainty. He also said concerning the children of Israel through the Prophet Isaiah:

> *I have not spoken in secret, In a corner of a land of darkness; I did not say to the descendants of Jacob, 'Seek Me in vain [with no benefit for yourselves].' I, the LORD, speak righteousness [the truth—trustworthy, a straightforward correlation between deeds and words], Declaring things that are upright.* (Isaiah 49:15 AMP)

God has not asked us to pray in vain, He wants us to pray to know that whatever we ask for, we will receive. God wants us to mix our prayer with faith—this is where most Christians miss it. Though they pray with hope, they are not expecting, nor do they trust that they will receive what they have asked for. In doing so, they have offered vain and idle words before God. Such prayers rarely get answered. God may honour such a prayer when you are new to salvation. However, as you grow up in Christ, such prayers do not go anywhere, because they are an affront to the principle of faith—the same principle with which the entire universe was formed and operates on.

According to the scripture, we cannot please God without faith. If we cannot please God without faith, then how can we expect Him to answer our faithless prayers? The truth is, not only will He not answer, but He can't—He does not hear it. God does not hear faithless prayers, because they are outside of His will (1 John 5: 14–15).

Praying with Faith

So the questions I am sure you are asking yourself are: How can I pray with certainty? Doesn't God choose the prayers He wants to answer? Didn't the Bible say we ask and we do not receive because we ask amiss? The answer to these questions is not really. The context in which James the brother of Jesus made this statement is addressing

Christians who were motivated by their fleshly desires. These are the Christians that asked amiss—the carnal Christians. The answer to this is what Jesus said:

> *If you abide in Me, and My words abide in you, you will ask what you desire, and it shall be done for you. By this My Father is glorified, that you bear much fruit; so you will be My disciples.* (John 15: 7 – 8 NKJV)

When we submit our desire to the authority of God's Word and allow the Holy Spirit to deal with our fleshly desires, our prayers will align with the will of God. Such prayers will always be answered by God. Always. However, we cannot submit ourselves to the authority of God's Word if we do not know Him. This is why Paul told the Roman Christians that faith comes by hearing God's Word (Romans 10:17). If you do not know His Word, you cannot submit to Him; if you do not submit to Him, you cannot pray according to His will; if you do not pray according to His will, He cannot hear you; if He does not hear you, then your prayers cannot be answered. Therefore, praying the right way starts with knowing and submitting to God's Word.

Call to Action

I will end this chapter as I started it. As Christians, we are mandated to pray. If we do not pray, Satan will have a free passage to wreak the havoc he intends unopposed. We must exercise God's authority on the Earth through prayer. Therefore, I am urging you to commit yourself to prayer—not prayer for what you want but to join the army of God (the Church) to pray the will of God on the Earth. You may think you are only one person, but we have learned from scripture that the fervent prayer of a righteous person avails much power. You owe it to yourself, your family, your community, your world and God, to pray. You have a unique role and responsibility. If you do not man your flank, you will allow Satan to attack through the void you have created. God is counting on you to rise to the occasion.

To the Church—we are only as strong as we are united. We are rapidly approaching the end of the Church age. What will our witness to God be at the rapture? It is our time to lead the world and, truth be told, the world is desperate for our leadership. However, we cannot lead if we are not unified under the Lordship of Jesus Christ. Therefore, God is calling us to the Seat of Truth, where we lay down our pride and dogma and submit to the Lordship of Jesus Christ with complete humility, so we can work together in love and unity. This is how Jesus intends for His body to function. It is my prayer that the messages in this book will be a contributing catalyst that lifts the Church from the mire of selfishness and carnality, brings us to our rightful place as the gods of the Earth under the Lordship of Jesus Christ.

Other Books
by Tolulope Oyewole

And they shall be called
the Sons of God

The Story of a Butterfly

Just Thinking

The Treasures of my Heart

A Word in Season

Printed in Great Britain
by Amazon

80303218R00062